CAPITALISM, DEMOCRACY & EMERGING CHRISTIANITY

An Essay By A Catholic Activist

STEPHEN V. RILEY

authorHOUSE®

AuthorHouse™
1663 Liberty Drive
Bloomington, IN 47403
www.authorhouse.com
Phone: 1-800-839-8640

First published by AuthorHouse 3/25/2010

ISBN: 978-1-4520-0568-3 (e)
ISBN: 978-1-4520-0567-6 (sc)

Library of Congress Control Number: 2010904083

Printed in the United States of America
Bloomington, Indiana

This book is printed on acid-free paper.

TO DEBORAH M. RILEY

This book is dedicated to Deborah, my loving wife of nearly forty-four years. She is the love of my life forever. To anyone who knew her, she was kind, vivacious, charming, smart, honest, and caring, and she always showed a great sense of humor.

In our earlier years, we were the builders and managers of our twenty-two-room Black Bear Lodge in Bolton Valley, Vermont. There we raised our two young children on skis. Debbie did most of the cooking at the Inn; she was always well-organized and a fabulous chef.

After our dinner seating, much like a private dinner party, Debbie would suddenly emerge from the kitchen to greet our guests, whipping off her apron—an elegantly dressed lady with a radiant smile.

We later moved to Florida, and Debbie returned to education, eventually becoming Assistant Director of the Sarasota Manatee Technical Institute in Bradenton, Florida. There she was loved by all her staff and was always supportive of the various departments: culinary, plumbing, electrical, fire academy, and nursing. As in the hospitality business, Debbie could work a room full of people like Tip O'Neil.

To me, Debbie was truly a living saint, particularly in how she dealt with my own personal shortcomings. Our greatest joys together were our two beautiful children, Stephenie and Allen, now in their early forties. It is really sad that Debbie never got to see her two grandchildren, Kaz and Sophia Sosnkowski, grow up in Lake Tahoe and ski-race with the young "Mighty Mites" at Squaw Valley.

IN GRATITUDE

I am grateful to Brian Fox, my trusted spiritual and financial advisor, who is a former social activist-videographer. Brian was a great support for me after the loss of my wife, Debbie. Brian is the person who encouraged me to publish this essay.

I am also thankful to Father Bill Nadeau, O. F. M., who is the pastor at St. Francis of Assisi Church in Incline Village, Nevada. He is a great priest who knows how to choose his words carefully in order to keep his flock together. If you had the ears to hear, you could always hear his progressive message. Father Bill could give a great homily, and he had a casual and nonecclesiastical demeanor. I loved to tease him by saying that he would make a lousy bishop.

My thanks also go to Franciscan Father Richard Rohr, founder of the Center for Action and Contemplation in Albuquerque, New Mexico. Father Richard has deepened my spirituality over the past three years. I would like to quote one of his daily reflections, one that reflects, in so many ways, my spiritual journey.

> Prayer is something that happens **to you** (Romans 8:26–27), much more than anything **you privately do**. It is an allowing of the Big Self more than an assertion of the small self. Eventually you will find yourself preferring to say, "Prayer happened, and I was there" more than "I prayed today." All you know is that you are being led, being guided, being loved, being used, being prayed through—and you are no longer in the driver's seat.

> God stops being an object of attention like any other object in the world and becomes at some level your own "I am". You start knowing through, with, and in Somebody Else. Your little "I am" becomes "We Are". Please trust me on this. It might be the most important thing I could tell you.

> (Richard Rohr, from "The Naked Now")

EMERGING CHRISTIANITY

The emerging Christianity movement, to my mind, is about a bold voice for universal justice. It is about the Christian obligation to seek a higher level of social awareness in order to reach an honest discernment of the spirits. It is about Christianity becoming a healing force in the world rather than a divisive force. It is about religious tolerance and encouraging dialogue and partnerships with other Christian denominations and other religions. To share one's sacred energies with people of other faiths takes humility and open-mindedness. The world desperately needs more of these attitudes.

My spiritual journey for peace and justice over the past ten years has led to deep social awareness and personal discernment. Great joy, hope, and personal fulfillment are found in sharing powerful energies with like-minded people of faith. Such sharing has always been a transformational experience for me.

This essay has been written as my own personal spiritual exercise to discern for myself where the emerging Christianity movement should be going. I am also compelled, however, to share some thoughts that go unarticulated in Christian conversations today. I believe that these thoughts should be articulated.

I believe the emerging Christianity movement is attracting like-minded people of faith who seek to invest their activist energies in a particular spiritual place, the place where they believe Christianity should be in the twenty-first century. Their quest is not about forming another denomination. There are enough divisions of faith. I believe many of the progressive faithful who choose to be part of the emerging Christianity movement are concerned with the increasing conservative forces within their own Christian denominations. Too many Christians are turning a blind eye to that wounded world where Jesus Christ, the Prince of Peace, showed humankind how to heal with love, compassion, and forgiveness.

A DIVIDED NATION AND A DIVIDED CHURCH

I believe the Catholic Church has become as divided and confused as the United States, and for many of the same reasons. Both view the world through the eyes of power, privilege, and wealth, and each has its own vision of empire. In turn, both the U.S. government and the Catholic Church are greatly divided by dominant conservative forces and struggling progressive forces. In both cases, the conservative forces are becoming less tolerant of dissenting viewpoints. These conservative forces are the great protectors of the unjust status quo. In contrast to this conservative stance, in coming to know the mind of Christ, one realizes that Christianity was meant to be a countercultural faith.

THE FUTURE CHURCH

John L. Allen, the astute Vatican observer and writer with the *National Catholic Reporter*, has recently authored a book, *The Future Church: How Ten Trends Are Revolutionizing the Catholic Church.* I have excerpted those thoughts that I believe are relevant to the development of the emerging Christianity movement.

Generally speaking, with strong influence from the global South, John Allen sees the Church becoming more conservative on moral questions such as abortion, homosexuality, and the family. However, in regard to economic, political, and military matters, the Church will be more liberal. Allen writes, "In non-Western nations, religious bodies are sometimes the only meaningful expressions of civil society—the only zones of life where protest can take shape, and where concern for the common good can be articulated."

John Allen speaks of the internal life of the Church as *ad intra* and the broader religious and social questions outside the Church as *ad extra*. To John Allen, the *ad extra* liberal camp is unlikely to make much headway in terms of setting *ad intra* policy. "On issue after issue, whether it's women priests or birth control, the tide is running decisively in the opposite position. He fears that

> "liberal reform movements in the twenty-first century will find themselves in a 'catacomb period' ... Given those realities, some progressive Catholics believe that their future lies in engaging social and political questions outside the church—shifting to *ad extra* rather than

ad intra causes … Ironically, the Catholic conservative identity impulse, which is by intent and design an *ad intra* phenomenon will likely have the effect of producing a boom period of *ad extra* Catholic activism."

John Allen points out that the aggressiveness of evangelical Catholicism and Pentecostalism will force the Catholic Church to a new imagination. This new imagination is that the Church will embrace more of the aspects of evangelical and Pentecostal Christianity and yet become ever more conservative and protective of its own distinctive Catholic identity. As John Allen writes, "there will be no dissent on the Church's payroll …" and "the Bishops will be the teachers-in-chief."

John Allen also brings up another important point. "If liberals are more likely to work in secular or ecumenical settings, to know the argot of modernity, and to know how to move the levers of social power outside the Catholic Church, they will arguably be in a better position to wield influence. Professional migration outside the Church may enhance the capacity of the Catholic left to build coalitions, and to argue persuasively with those who are not formed by the Catholic tradition. Ironically, evangelical Catholicism could end up giving a boost to the social capital of Catholic liberalism."

John L. Allen discusses, as well, how the Catholic Church's hierarchical mode of operation may lack the flexibility needed to keep up with the intense pace at which issues mutate in a globalized world. "To expect the hierarchy to be the primary "change agent" is both unfair and unrealistic. … Radical change has to well up from grass roots activism. …Ultimately, time and the tides stop for no one, and good ideas will endure whatever their initial reception by the powers that be." John Allen makes another powerful point when he states, "The real question, therefore, is not whether the bishops are up to the challenges of the 21st century. The question is whether the rest of us are." The *us*, to me, means all Christian denominations.

The future direction of the Catholic Church that John Allen writes about certainly provides more than a few thoughts that are fertile ground for an emerging Christianity movement. I stress, however, that I believe John Allen has overlooked the influence of a higher social consciousness that is rapidly developing in the world. It is a far more powerful force for radical social change than the "exclusive" forces of Catholicism can now play. I believe the Catholic Church feels threatened by this secular force, not humbled by its powerful spirituality. This is understandable, considering the ego of any institution accustomed to such power and control. For these reasons, I believe the emerging Christianity movement will find its own humble place in recognizing this emerging higher global consciousness as the work of the Holy Spirit and become an influential partner in this fast-developing shift in global consciousness.

BLESSED UNREST

This emerging global consciousness is best described in Paul Hawken's book *Blessed Unrest, How the Largest Social Movement in History Is Restoring Grace, Justice, and Beauty to the World.* Paul Hawken has given nearly one thousand talks about the environment to hundreds of thousands of people who are working on climate change, poverty, deforestation, peace, water, hunger, conservation, and human rights. They come from the nonprofit and nongovernment world known as civil society. Paul Hawken estimates there could be as many as one to two million organizations in the world that are working toward ecological sustainability and social justice. The movement, though, doesn't fit the standard model, as it has no manifesto or doctrine, no overriding authority. It is almost mysterious, a sacred act emerging as a global humanitarian movement arising from the bottom up. It is engaged in protecting citizens, workers, and environments from the juggernaut of free market fundamentalism. Paul Hawken refers to this movement as the Blessed Unrest.

Paul Hawken looks at the entire movement from two perspectives: that of "immunity" and that of environment and social justice. "Immunity" uses the cellular metaphor of how an organism defends itself as a plausible way to describe the collective activity of the movement The terms *environment* and *social justice* encompass innovative organizations that are redolent of ideas and inventive techniques.

"Nature works in cycles and so does a healthy society. A self-correcting system thrives because of feedback. The movement is composed of small organizations because it is on the ground, with its people at the scene—a scale at which information can be generated and acted upon. At this level, organizations quickly adapt. Mistakes are hidden treasures because we learn from our failures. The opposite of learning is a runaway system where mistakes are relegated to file cabinets and ignored. When government, corporation, financial institution, or religious organization insulates itself, its initiatives, however well intended, create uncontrolled outcomes and second order effects that generate new problems. The current state of the world reflects a problem solving methodology never seen in nature: remedies from above imposed on the excluded. The movement offers a solution creating methodology from below that is inclusive, a process that mimics biological adaptation and evolution. Every physical activity of the human body sustains is part of a cyclical, biological system with a self-correcting bias. The same should be true of every social activity with a system called democracy."

THE FIRST EMERGING CHRISTIANITY CONFERENCE

The first conference then called "emerging church" was held in March 2009 at the Center of Action and Contemplation in Albuquerque,

New Mexico. (www.cacradicalgrace.org). There were about a thousand people in attendance, and about half were Catholic; the other half were from about twenty-five denominations. The conference presenters were well-known Christian scholars. Many of their thoughts had been previously presented in the CAC *Radical Grace* publication (October-December 2008, vol. 21, no. 4).

About a hundred and fifty people attended the immediate postconference discussion, and I sensed that about half were active clergy from many denominations. This meeting was about a cornucopia of thoughts and ideas stimulating the convergence of like-minded people of faith. The conference concluded with a very appropriate Thomas Merton prayer.

My Lord God, I have no idea where I am going. I do not see the road ahead of me. I cannot know for certain where it will end. Nor do I really know myself, and the fact that I think I am following your will does not mean that I am actually doing so. But I believe that the desire to please you does in fact please you. And I hope I have that desire in all that I am doing. I hope that I will never do anything apart from that desire. And I know that if I do this you will lead me by the right road though I may know nothing about it. Therefore I will trust you always though I may seem to be lost and in the shadow of death. I will not fear, for you are ever with me, and you will never leave me to face my perils alone.

The next emerging Christianity conference is scheduled for April 9–11, 2010, at the Center of Action and Contemplation in Albuquerque, New Mexico. It will be most interesting; everyone will be anxious to get clearer sense of its direction. It is my hope that the emerging Christianity movement will become a Christian vanguard for a higher social awareness and a progressive force for radical social change. Certainly, though, there will be many other suggestions.

In the first conference, there was much discussion about the faithful being more prophetic and contemplative. Being prophetic is about the role Christians need to play in healing a broken world. It is to do the very work of the Hebrew prophets and a willingness to see through new eyes and not content to be silent. As Sister Joan Chittister often says, we're in this mess because we no longer have any Isaiahs, Esichias, Samuels, or Malachis to set us straight. So I see prophecy as a vital component of emerging Christianity. In turn, Christ was all about healing and driving out demons. We must now recognize the demons within our own humanity, the human ego, and the demons within the American capitalistic culture.

By being contemplative, we try to recognize our own human shortcomings. In contemplation, we deal with our inner violence, which is the work of the human ego. At times the personal ego can be our worst enemy, expressing itself in vanity, pride, arrogance, envy, exaggerated individualism, the lust for power and wealth, rage, violence, war, scapegoating others, the need to be right, and the *me against you* and *us against them* mentalities. The dysfunctional nature of the personal ego is addressed by the foundational teachings of most of the major religions of the world. Christ had the perfect nonegotistic mind. Christ also had a hard time getting this point across to the minds of his disciples.

In a September 4, 2009, article in the *National Catholic Reporter*, Father Richard Rohr, founder of the Center of Action and Contemplation, stated that another term for *contemplation* is *non-*

dualistic thinking. "That's what makes people able to be merciful and forgiving. You can't love your enemies with a low level dualistic mind. It's impossible. You don't have the software to know how to do it. So we tell people to love your enemies. A normal Catholic can't do that with the software that he or she has been given. Catholics were never taught they need a different consciousness to understand the Gospel." I so often reflect on Richard Rohr's wise words from past conferences—"Christianity has become a belonging system, us against them, rather than a system for personal transformation." Emerging Christianity should be increasingly conscious of this contradiction.

Meditation and contemplation are the best ways to overcome the dominance of the personal ego, at least partially, at times. Meditation becomes a quest for wisdom by putting oneself in the Presence, in deep prayer, setting aside one's personal interest and seeking wisdom though spiritual discernment. With much practice in meditation and contemplation, spiritual discernment can become a gift of the Holy Spirit. To me, spiritual discernment is the essential path to the maturity of humankind. This path teaches us that everything is not black or white. It cautions us that one cannot be tied down by all-knowing absolutes.

DEMOCRACY, SPIRITUALITY, AND NONVIOLENT CIVIL DISOBEDIENCE

The civic challenge of democracy is a somewhat similar spiritual exercise. The vast majority of the U.S. Congress and federal government agency leaders are led by huge egos and questionable obligations to the powerful. In the U.S. Congress, those who lead with wisdom and honest personal discernment can be counted on one hand. The majority of the U.S. Congress is simply not free to think great thoughts for the common good. This is why the spiritual dynamics of participatory democracy are so important for a free society. A healthy democracy is meant to bring about a public consensus and discernment that questions the controlling forces of institutional power.

But public awareness and discernment has been seriously hindered by a corporate TV and news media that relies exclusively on advertising. This tips the scales to favor corporate interests and corporate spin. The lack of public awareness is also reinforced by a corporate media that controls the national conversation and distracts American society with unrelenting entertainment. Neal Postman speaks of this so well in his book, *Amusing Ourselves to Death: Public Discourse in the Age of Show Business.*

THE SPIRITUAL DYNAMICS OF DEMOCRACY

The freedom of democracy is also threatened by a complacent society. Certainly the financial upper third of the U.S. population has difficulty questioning a system that has "so blessed them." It is difficult for the "successful" to think in terms of the common good. Such material success flatters the personal ego. Because of this, a dangerous form of consumer elitism has emerged in the United States—an elitism that has a condescending disdain for the democratic rule of the majority.

War is the greatest danger to a democratic society because it shifts national priorities and national resources away from the social good. When alert citizens see a dangerous and unjust fork in the road and feel the government has turned a deaf ear to their pleas, then active, nonviolent civil disobedience is most certainly in order. To me, creative, nonviolent civil disobedience is an obligation on the part of both honest democracy and honest Christianity.

But civic faith in the power of democracy in the United States has been seriously weakened. Too few citizens have the freedom and passion to engage in nonviolent civil disobedience. Some sense they have too much to lose by such action. They are not free to do so because they have bought fully into the system. However, increasing numbers of American citizens are beginning to feel powerless. Their hope for a better life and a more peaceful and just society has become a broken American dream.

These people have forgotten the power of democratic hope. They have forgotten that the teachings of Christ are about hope for a more just world. Christian hope is what drove the civil rights movement. That movement had the powerful imagination to see all men as equal. This was Dr. Martin Luther King's "I have a dream" speech. American apathy is a danger to democracy and the public good. U.S. citizens should never lose sight of the fact that the U.S. government fears democratic activism and creative nonviolent civil disobedience because it works. It works because of the unconquerable power **of the human spirit and the human imagination.**

UNDER THE SPELL OF CORPORATE CAPITALISM

On January 21, 2010, the Supreme Court issued a ruling in *Citizens United v. the Federal Elections Commission*. This 'free speech' decision in favor of unlimited corporate spending in political campaigns is expected to have dire consequences for the equal, democratic involvement and influence of U.S. citizens in the politics of their own country.

This ruling of the Supreme Court only reaffirms the unspoken fact that corporate capitalism has literal control over American society and the U.S. Congress. The choices of consumer capitalism have become the substitute for American democracy. To the ruling oligarchs of corporate capitalism, democratic rule for the common good is no less an evil than socialism or communism. To them, there is to be no compromise with the ideology of corporate free market capitalism.

I believe corporate capitalism has proven to be the enemy of Christianity as well. Consumer capitalism has corrupted American Christianity by hardening the human heart, suppressing the human spirit, and promoting the deceitful gospel of prosperity. To overcome the forces of corporate capitalism, Christianity must align itself with the forces of democracy. Granted, democracy is relatively new to Christianity, but democracy can be just as much an act of the human spirit as the practice of religion, and without the threat of theocracy. This is now being learned in Central and South America and throughout the world. But it is not without its problems. For example, under the cover of a weak democracy, but with government repudiation of U.S. corporate imperialism, Venezuela is still ruled by cronyism and corruption under the near-dictatorship of Hugo Chavez.

THE POOR ARE BECOMING SUFFICIENTLY AWARE

With instant world-wide communications, the world's poor now need not be oppressed by what they do not know. The poor are becoming sufficiently aware that corporate imperialism is the major cause of their oppression. They are now moved by a hunger for justice. To quote Paul Hawken: "There has always been networks of powerful people, but until recently, it has never been possible for the entire world to be connected ... Rather than seeking dominance, this unnamed movement strives to disperse concentrations of power. ... Its clout resides in its ideas, not in force."

But the future challenges for radical social change are enormous. The ruling capitalists are terrified of such a shift in global consciousness. So they cleverly turn their fear around and manipulate the American people with fear. That is the whole purpose of the Patriot Act and the Department of Homeland Security. The U.S. government is going to great lengths to prepare for this universal shift in social consciousness by increasing the powers of the National Security State and equipping local police forces to suppress nearly all forms of democratic dissent. The ruling corporatists are desperate to protect the corporate empire and its ideologies of free market capitalism that only make the rich richer and the poor poorer. It may be unsettling to say, but the CIA was founded primarily to protect the interests of Wall Street. So again, the future challenges for radical social change are enormous.

The emerging Christianity movement needs to recognize that multinational corporate capitalism has become the new imperialism of the world. It is a totalitarian force that is a threat to humankind. It is the elephant in the living room that no one wants to speak about. The emerging Christianity movement should be a bold voice that dares to speak about this issue. Otherwise, I believe, the emerging Christianity movement will never become a viable force for radical social change.

THE BEGINNING OF MY SPIRITUAL JOURNEY

My passion for social justice activism began twelve years ago. At that time, I read *When Corporations Rule the World* by David Korten. It was a very powerful read for me. It transformed my views of the United States and the world. It greatly challenged me to broaden my faith in a spiritual way. I found a deep underlying spiritual message in David Korten's writing, which resonated with the spirit of subsidiarity. The term *subsidiarity* is a relatively unknown principle of Catholic social teaching that is about avoiding any economic activity on a higher level that can be done on a local level in order to maintain the economic vitality of the local community.

David Korten has since written three additional books: *The Post Corporate World: Life After Capitalism, The Great Turning: From Empire to Earth Community*, and, most recently, *Agenda to A New Economy: From Phantom Wealth to Real Wealth.* His *Agenda to a New Economy* was appropriately launched in January 2009 at a conference hosted by the Episcopal Wall Street Church, which is located just across the street from the New York Stock Exchange.

My reading of *When Corporations Rule the World* led me to three particular books among others that would deepen my awareness early in my spiritual journey. They are as follows.

***Stolen Harvest: The Hijacking of The Global Food Supply* by Vandana Shiva.** I was fortunate to be there to hear Vandana Shiva and Ralph Nader debate three multinational corporate CEOs at a teach-in by the International Forum on Globalization in Seattle at the time of the WTO demonstrations. It was like two Jesuits debating grammar school kids. As a physicist, Dr. Vandana Shiva is by far the most renowned international expert and activist speaking against the multinational corporate agribusiness model that is disrupting the small farmers' economies all over the world and equally so in her native India. Her book *Stolen Harvest* awakened the world, much like Rachel Carson's *Silent Spring*.

Shaking the Gates of Hell: Faith Led Resistance to Globalization by Sharon Delgado. Unlike David Korten's book *When Corporations Rule the World*, this book has not been widely read and is heavily based on Scripture. It deserves to be read by every person of faith. I would later write an Amazon book review on *Shaking the Gates of Hell* and another twelve Amazon book reviews.

Alternatives to Economic Globalization: A Better World Is_Possible by Jerry Mander and John Cavanagh. This book was initiated by the International Forum on Globalization, an international economic think tank and a teaching institution on the issues of corporate globalization.

WORKING FOR A JUST, SUSTAINABLE, AND COMPASSIONATE WORLD

As mentioned earlier, democratic activism is really a passionate act of the human spirit, and it should be an important part of the emerging church movement. Broadly speaking, it should be about working for a more just, sustainable, and compassionate world. It is Christianity serving as praxis to an emerging higher global consciousness. This emerging higher global consciousness is also seen as the evolutionary destiny of humankind in providing for its own survival. It is about "the great turning" that the Buddhist scholar Joanna Macy speaks about. It is radical because it takes the mechanism of how the world works and turns that mechanism on its head. It is about ways of doing business that support local communities. Humankind is now learning that local communities are far more sustainable than "corporatizing" the world economy and far less vulnerable to economic bubbles and meltdowns, as recently experienced with the collapse of Wall Street in 2008. Many Christians may also view this emerging higher consciousness as the incarnate spirit of the risen Christ that now dwells within all of humankind.

A NEW EARTH

In *A New Earth, Awakening to Your Life's Purpose*, Eckhart Tolle writes about how the love of money and the love of things can contribute to the domination of the human ego and how a consumer society honors material things as a means of self-enhancement. The love of things distorts our perception of reality and the true nature of our humanity.

Eckhart Tolle expressed that essential distortion so well: "Ego-identification with things creates attachment to things, obsession with things, which in turn creates our consumer society and economic structures where the only measure of progress is always more. The unchecked striving for more, for endless growth, is a dysfunction and a disease. It is the same dysfunction the cancerous cell manifests, whose only goal is to multiply itself, unaware that it is bringing about its own destruction by destroying the organism of which it is a part."

AWAKENING THE DREAMER, CHANGING THE DREAM

In regard to the unsustainable appetite for economic growth by corporate capitalism and the emerging higher global consciousness, I love the commentary by a web site obviously influenced by the writings of Paul Hawken. It is called Awakening the Dreamer, Changing the Dream.

I quote: "The world seems to be spinning ever faster toward disaster through climate change, warfare, disease, famine and financial meltdown. We could be forgiven for reacting with denial, despair or despondency, and some people are. Yet simultaneously the largest ever social movement in history is rising up to resist the forces causing these crises and to build a world that works sustainably for all life."

"This is arguably the biggest story of our age; how tens of millions of people in millions of organizations around the world are recognizing that our current ways are dysfunctional, they are seeing sustainable, peaceful and just alternatives and standing up for their visions. In many cases this means standing up to governments, corporations or the peer pressure that seeks to perpetuate our present worldview."

The commentary continues, "When a caterpillar reaches a certain point in its own evolution, it becomes over-consumptive, a voracious eater and it eats everything in sight.

"At that same time, in the molecular structure of the caterpillar, the "imaginal cells" become active. While all this gorging is going on, those imaginal cells wake up, and they look for each other inside of the caterpillar's body. When enough of them connect (they don't need to be in the majority) they become the genetic directors of the future of the caterpillar. At that point the other cells begin to putrefy and become what's called the nutritive soup—out of which the imaginal cells create the absolute unpredictable miracle of the butterfly.

"What's possible is that we're the imaginal cells on the planet right now."

THE NEED FOR A NEW NATIONAL CONVERSATION

To most Americans, the idea that the nature of institutional capitalism is an unsustainable cancer to our nation and the world is the most unthinkable thought. It is time Americans begin to shift their thinking in new ways. Presently the God of capitalism is efficiency, and its fuel is greed. It is the efficiency to maximize profits while disregarding the true costs of human dignity. Consumer capitalism also makes its money by tempting and feeding on the weaknesses of the human ego. The selfish dynamics of capitalism make for a dysfunctional society. Certainly, by now, it must be seen that Wall Street has become little more than a system of financial chicanery and deceit. There seems to be no room left for diligent moral scrutiny. The United States needs a deep introspection, a new imagination, and a new national conversation. The emerging Christianity movement should become the stimulating force to a new national conversation.

GETTING THE MESSAGE OF CHRIST AFTER TWO THOUSAND YEARS

Christianity in America has been tiptoeing through the tulips of corporate capitalism for too long. The destiny of Christian Americans is to be more honest to their Christian faith now. They must choose to be more like the early Christians, who rejected the predominant culture of their time and saw through new eyes, the eyes of Christ. It was Jesus, the radical revolutionary, who preached against unjust institutions of power and money. Everything Jesus preached was politically subversive and dangerous. This included his criticism of excessive mercantilism, religious hypocrisy, the oppression of the poor by the rich, the excessive interest rates of usury, and the Roman Empire's wars of conquest. .Do any of these issues sound like problems we confront presently?

One can see that, other than stupendous leaps in technology, little has changed in two thousand years. The teachings of Christ have been pretty much ignored. Rather than investing in personal spiritual transformation to heal the world, people of power and money chose to put all their faith in the creative powers of technologies for increasing the pleasures and comforts for people, though only for those who can afford those technologies. Over time, this activity took place pretty much at the expense of the greater part of humanity and the natural environment. Unfortunately, this included creative technologies for warfare that are being turned back upon the forces of empire in the world today, such as the United States of America.

But a higher consciousness is emerging in the world, a consciousness that recognizes the immense power of the human spirit and every person's natural right and desire for human dignity. This emerging higher consciousness is signaling a maturation of humankind. To me, it is the working of the Holy Spirit. This higher consciousness is coming from the people below, not from the powerful rulers at the top. As the world becomes smaller and more interrelated and interconnected, the need for deep personal transformation and the creative powers of the human spirit becomes more evident. This awakening of humankind sees that the survival of the human species depends upon the unifying and healing powers of human compassion. It has taken humankind two thousand years to begin to understand the teachings of Christ. **God works in mysterious ways.**

THE MACHINERY OF WAR IS PURE MADNESS

Defending the United States against terrorist attacks is futile when the root causes of terrorism are continually ignored. That disregard is an attitude that I call blind madness. The mainstream media is obsessed with the threats of terrorism but remains clueless about the roots of terrorism. The CIA, the Pentagon, the U.S. National Security State, and the U.S. military industrial complex are the institutions that promote this national blindness. Our nation's limited imagination of capitalistic technology and warfare to heal a broken world is the foundation for stupidity. The greed of Wall Street is the great cheerleader. This all reminds me of a common Vietnam vet saying, "We had to destroy the village in order to save it." Today, in a very similar way, we are destroying our nation in order to protect it.

IN THE PRESENCE OF FEAR

In his book *In the Presence of Fear*, Wendell Berry, the well-known author, poet, social critic, and Kentucky farmer, presented his now famous twenty-seven reflections in the aftermath of 9/11. This pamphlet-sized book is available at http://www.orionmagazine.org/index.php/article/214.

Wendell Berry's first three reflections are as follow.

I. The time will soon come when we will not be able to remember the horrors of September 11 without remembering also the unquestioning technological and economic optimism that ended on that day.

II. This optimism rested on the proposition that we were living in a "new world order" and a "new economy" that would "grow" on and on, bringing a prosperity of which every new increment would be "unprecedented."

III. The dominant politicians, corporate officers, and investors who believed this proposition did not acknowledge that the prosperity was limited to a tiny percent of the world's people, and to a smaller number of people even in the United States; that it was founded upon the oppressive labor of poor people all over the world; and that its ecological costs increasingly threatened all life, including the lives of the supposedly prosperous.

AMERICAN MILITARY POWER

The Roman Empire in Christ's time was certainly a violent and bloody oppressive force. The imperialistic empire of our day is certainly more sanitized with the oppression of global financial markets and the monopoly of industrial capitalism. This subtler violence, however, is backed up by brutal American military power.

American military power in today's world raises many questions. Why is national patriotism only about war? Why is our nation so accepting of the huge military budget? Is the American defense industry becoming our new national industry? Shouldn't the increasing power of the National Security State be seen as a threat to democratic rule and democratic dissent? How is it possible for overwhelming military power to squash the human spirit? How can military power bring democracy to a nation at the point of a gun? How can bombing civilians bring peace when it only encourages more terrorists?

More and more people are coming to believe that war is futile, that war is now obsolete. The indisputable fact is that war has always been deceitfully sold by governments through propaganda that scapegoats others and questions personal patriotism. Emerging Christianity should be speaking about these issues. Many religious scholars are becoming aware that the war on terrorism is really a clash between the materialistic forces of global corporate capitalism and the forces of spirituality. The forces of spirituality are a cry for human liberation from economic oppression and a cry for universal justice.

THE ARROGANCE OF CORPORATE CAPITALISM

Corporate capitalism has such arrogance that it even seeks to control and profit on all aspects of human life. It wants to turn all essential human endeavors into commodities to be sold just so that it can make ever more money. A few good examples are privatizing many aspects of the military, privatizing the rights to water, privatizing the rights to healthcare, privatizing the prison system and the education system, controlling the news media, and patterning genetically modified seeds and the biological makeup of all forms of life. These actions amount to robbery of the entire human community.

This is unbelievable when you really think about it. Consumer capitalism is altering human consciousness. Global capitalism is ripping apart local communities and is corrupting democracies by destroying the social state and national sovereignties all over the world. It denies nations the ability to determine their own economic destiny. It is destroying local family farming while the world starves. Corporate capitalism has poisoned our food and our water and poisoned our bodies as well. Corporate capitalism is a beast that is out of control, and it will ultimately destroy the world by overconsumption unless alternative systems are put in its place. Corporations should not be ruling the world. People and democracy should be ruling the world.

STRUCTURAL EVIL

To take a purely technical approach, corporate capitalism has a structure that is intrinsically evil. It is the evil that emanates from publically traded corporations. These corporations are under tremendous pressure by Wall Street financial speculators and hedge funds. These corporations are forced to produce ever-increasing shareholder value. In laymen's terms, this is about making wealthy stockholders ever wealthier. But wealth is not the real problem. The problem is that the system becomes dehumanizing. Stockholder value becomes the sole ruthless driving force of corporations, which relentlessly reduce the cost of labor and externalize as many costs as possible onto society. Human values, healthy foods, the sacredness of the Earth, and the vitality of local communities become meaningless in such a harsh, competitive capitalistic society.

THE FORGIVENESS OF CHRIST IS THE POWER TO CHANGE THE WORLD

Emerging Christianity should be mainly about how forgiveness and loving your enemy can change the world.

At the risk of appearing blasphemous, Father Richard Rohr shared an unusual analogy at a previous CAC conference. The analogy is not as beautiful as that of the butterfly, but it is equally as transformative.

The large steel-grey electrical transformers commonly seen on wooden utility poles are designed to receive extremely high voltage from a power plant and reduce this energy into a less violent form for use in the home. In a similar way, on the cross, Christ received and transformed within his own body the violent energies of the world into the peaceful energy of love, forgiveness, and compassion. We ourselves now must become like Christ, absorbing and transforming the violence in the world within ourselves to bring forth love, forgiveness and compassion to the world. Personal transformation requires the inner work of meditation, contemplation, and discernment.

THOUGHTS ON 9/11

The perfect example of reaction to violence with violence was the second human tragedy of 9/11. The United States could have reacted differently. Like the electrical transformer and the way of Christ on the cross, America could have transformed that violence into a more peaceful energy. Our nation could have reacted as we have always done with crime in our neighborhoods—with patient and determined police action. We could have called upon the community of nations and Islam itself for justice through international police action.

But this is not an impractical fantasy that the warmongers wanted us to believe. The reality was that nearly the entire world was ready and willing to participate in such police action. But powerful forces in the American government had a hidden agenda and chose to wage two wars in Afghanistan and Iraq. These forces wanted to prove that the United States could unilaterally work its will in the world as it saw fit, and they exploited people's fears of terrorism to do so.

THOUGHTS OF LIBERATION THEOLOGY

With my thoughts on the emerging Christianity movement, I can't help but recall the Brazilian priest, Franciscan Father Leonardo Boff, one of the leading Catholic theologians of our times. His teachings on liberation theology have made the Catholic Church rather uncomfortable because his doctrine threatens the dominance of Western financial and industrial capitalism.

Please allow me to quote these excerpts from the introduction of Leonardo Boff's book *Cry of the Earth, Cry of the Poor.*

The Earth is also crying out. The logic that exploits classes and subjects peoples to the interests of a few rich and powerful countries is the same as the logic that devastates the Earth and plunders its wealth, showing no solidarity with the rest of humankind and future generations.

It is not only the poor and oppressed that must be liberated; today all humans must be liberated. We are hostages to a paradigm that places us—against the thrust of the universe—over things instead of being with them in the great cosmic community.

The new paradigm that is coming to birth—that of connectedness—will be the basis of a universal religion that will only be truly universal if it seeks convergences in religious diversity. The convergences to be achieved must have to do with restoring the sacredness of all things, reclaiming the dignity of Earth, rediscovering the mission of the human being—man and women—called to celebrate the mystery of the cosmos, and finally, encountering God, mystery of communion and life, in the process of cosmogenesis itself. In embracing the world, we will be embracing God.

In *Future Church*, John Allen addressed, at least partially, the issues of liberation theology: "Another danger for the Church in the twenty-first century is that much creative energy could be stifled, not on its merits, but rather due to suspicions of a slippery slope leading to confusion about Church identity. One sees this today in Latin America, for example, in continuing ambivalence about "base ecclesial communities," meaning small groups of faithful who come together for prayer, worship, and social analysis. Some liberation theologians in the 1970s and 1980s saw the base communities as a "church from below" in opposition to the hierarchy as a "church from above." To John Allen, the rise of these base ecclesial communities tripped the "identity wire" of the Catholic Church.

It is unfortunate that liberation theology has been so stigmatized by economic conservative Christians. The thinking of Leonardo Boff is about interpreting scripture through the eyes of the poor, not through the eyes of the wealth and power. As well, Leonardo Boff's thinking is well-aligned with the emerging global consciousness that we are discussing. This higher consciousness is also an issue upon which the great thinkers of the social transformation of our times, such as David Korten, Paul Hawken, Hazel Henderson, Duane Elgin, Joanna Macy, and the late Thomas Berry, have written.

THE EARTH CHARTER

The social architecture of this emerging consciousness is contained in the Earth Charter, one of the greatest social documents ever written in the history of mankind.

The preamble of the Earth Charter states that "We stand at a critical moment in Earth's history, a time when humanity must choose its future. As the world becomes increasingly interdependent and fragile, the future at once holds great peril and great promise. To move forward we must recognize that in the midst of a magnificent diversity of cultures and life forms we are one human family and one Earth community with a common destiny. We must join together to bring forth a sustainable global society founded on respect for nature, universal human rights, economic justice, and a culture of peace. Towards this end, it is imperative that we, the peoples of Earth, declare our responsibility to one another, to the greater community of life, and to future generations."

The Earth Charter was voted down by the UN, primarily by the United States., as a threat to Western industrial capitalism. There are also fundamentalist Christians who are threatened by the spirituality of the Earth Charter. They err in relating it to the "end of times" theory that will see a system of global government and one-world religion employed by the Antichrist to deceive the faithful. Unfortunately the Earth Charter initiative within the United Nations is temporarily sidelined by the war on terrorism. The emerging Christianity movement should be an advocate for the Earth Charter initiative. .

THE CIA AND THE US MILITARY INDUSTRIAL COMPLEX

Hidden powers in America are determined to rule the world. Such desire drives the American Empire. James Douglass speaks of this desire in his book *JFK and the Unspeakable: Why He Died and Why It Matters.* Jim Douglass is a longtime peace activist and writer and a Catholic theologian of peace. He provides the reader with startling revelations of the unlimited powers of the CIA, an organization that sees itself as unaccountable to anyone. The National Security Act of 1947 laid the foundations of a National Security State by way of directive NSC 10/2 and its crimes, to be covered, if necessary, by the national security doctrine of "plausible deniability."

With sixteen years of research, newly released documents, tapes, and intimate discussions with close associates of John F. Kennedy, James Douglass describes how young John F. Kennedy was greatly pressured by the CIA and the joint chiefs of staff not to entertain any thoughts of ending the Cold War with Russia. After being misled and trapped by the CIA in the Bay of Pigs invasion, John Kennedy was transformed from a cold warrior to a warrior for peace. As a result, he wanted "to splinter the CIA in a thousand pieces and scatter it to the winds."

As James Douglass saw it, John F. Kennedy had undergone a deep personal transformation. But he found himself opening a wider chasm between himself and his own military and intelligence advisors by virtue of this transformation. President Kennedy was stunned by the utter stupidity and madness of the joint chiefs of staff, who wanted to bomb the Russian missiles in Cuba and risk unleashing a nuclear war. In the case of the Bay of Pigs and the Russian missiles in Cuba, these "intelligence" advisors had strategically counted on the new president to fold under pressure and thus fulfill their hidden strategic plans. They were totally shocked by Kennedy's bold and determined resistance. "They figured me wrong," said John F. Kennedy.

During this time, the contemplative monk Thomas Merton was challenging the Cold War dogmas with his correspondence to a number of people of great influence, including Ethel Kennedy and Clare Boothe Luce. Pope John XXIII had also released his encyclical *Pacem in Terris* ("Peace on Earth"). We have no way of knowing for sure how much Thomas Merton and Pope John XXIII had influenced President Kennedy. But his later American University speech certainly reflects that distinct possibility.

President John F. Kennedy was at war with much of the U.S. "Cold War" military and intelligence establishment, and the hostility continued, with John Kennedy refusing a military acceleration in Laos and Vietnam and a deadly confrontation with the Soviet Union over the Berlin Wall. John F. Kennedy also faced additional hostility from the steel industry because he had denied them their proposed price increases, and this action put big business in great fear of increasing government control. These interests believed that our nation should be solely left in the hands of big business.

The final blow to the military and intelligence establishment came when John F. Kennedy delivered his little-known Commencement Address on June 10, 1963, at the American University in Washington, DC. He proposed, in effect, to end the Cold War. This address was not very well-covered by the U.S. mainstream media. However, President Kennedy's address appeared in full on the front pages of almost every newspaper in the Soviet Union.

The Cold War warriors now believed John F. Kennedy to be a traitor to U.S. interests. In retrospect, however, he most certainly saved the world from nuclear war. President Kennedy introduced his subject to the graduating class as "the most important topic on earth: world peace." John Kennedy publically confronted and resisted the CIA, the National Security State, and U.S. military industrial complex. He did so in this speech. He was the first and only American president to do so.

John F. Kennedy's American University Commencement Address proclaimed to the world that a national self-examination by the United States was needed as the first step to world peace. Certainly a part of John Kennedy's address was in response to his private conversations with Nikita Khrushchev. In his American University address, John Kennedy was writing "Profiles in Courage" all over again. At least once a year, this commencement address should be read from every pulpit in the America.

On November 21, 1963, before leaving for Texas and after being given a list of the most recent casualties in Vietnam, President Kennedy said to Assistant Press Secretary Malcolm Kilduff: "After I come back from Texas, that's going to change. Vietnam is not worth another American life."

John F. Kennedy's continuing war with the CIA and the Joint Chiefs of Staff ended with his assassination on November 22, 1963. The former CIA director Allen Dulles, whom John F. Kennedy had quietly fired, was appointed by the new president, Lyndon Johnson, to serve on the Warren Commission that was investigating the assassination of John F. Kennedy.

At the end of this essay is the text of President John F. Kennedy's American University Commencement Address. I am sure the reader will find it just as powerful and relevant, if not more, as when that speech was given nearly fifty years ago.

DR. MARTIN LUTHER KING, THE PROPHET OF HIS TIME

The most prophetic message by Dr Martin Luther King was his declaration that "a nation that continues year after year to spend more money on military defense than on programs of social uplift is approaching spiritual death." This was in his April 4, 1967, speech in Riverside Church, New York City. It was titled "Beyond Vietnam: a Time to Break Silence." To this day, the mainstream media has ignored the Riverside speech, preferring to define Dr. King by his more famous "I Have a Dream" speech. The media does so to overshadow his transformation from a civil rights leader to an advocate for peace. Martin Luther King criticized the American military industrial establishment when he said, "The United States is the greatest purveyor of violence in the world today." The Riverside speech was a courageous but dangerous speech that marked him for assignation, just as President John F. Kennedy's Commencement Address at American University marked its author.

ROBERT F. KENNEDY JR.

Robert Kennedy shared the experience of personal transformation for peace with his brother, President John F. Kennedy. After his brother's assassination, Robert F. Kennedy continued to serve as attorney general under President Lyndon B. Johnson. After only six months, Kennedy resigned to seek the U.S. Senate seat from New York, which he won in November. It was then that he publicly split with Johnson over the Vietnam War.

In March 1968, Kennedy began a campaign for the presidency. Robert Kennedy then defeated Eugene McCarthy in the Democratic Primary. Following a brief victory speech delivered just past midnight on June 5, 1968, at the Ambassador Hotel in Los Angeles, Robert Kennedy was assassinated.

My favorite RFK quotation comes from Robert Kennedy's speech in Capetown, South Africa, on June 6, 1966. I find this speech most applicable to the emerging Christianity movement.

"Give me a lever and place to stand," said Archimedes, "and I will move the world."

... These men (civil rights activists in South Africa) moved the world, and so can we all. Few will have the greatness to bend history itself, but each of us can work to change a small portion of events, and in the total of all those acts will be written the history of this generation. Thousands of Peace Corps volunteers are making a difference in isolated villages and city slums in dozens of countries. Thousands of unknown men and women in Europe resisted the occupation of the Nazis and many died, but all added to the ultimate strength and freedom of their countries. It is from numberless diverse acts of courage and belief that human history is shaped. Each time a man stands up for an ideal, or acts to improve the lot of others, or strikes out against injustice, he sends forth a tiny ripple of hope, and crossing each other from a million different centers of energy and daring those ripples build a current which can sweep down the mightiest walls of oppression and resistance.

Robert Kennedy concluded that speech with the words of his brother, President John F. Kennedy: "With a good conscience our only sure reward, with history the final judge of our deeds, let us go forth to lead the land we love, asking His blessing and His help, but knowing that here on earth God's work must truly be our own."

As I reflect on the assassinations of John F. Kennedy, Martin Luther King, and Robert F. Kennedy, I can't help but think of the current Obama administration and the continuing wars in Iraq and Afghanistan. I question what these assassinations should mean to the American people. I have concluded that President Obama cannot challenge the powers that be in America without his life being threatened. He cannot afford to challenge the military industrial establishment alone.

As American citizens, we must finally come to understand there will be no end to wars by the United States until millions of American people have the courage to resist war boldly, with massive and creative nonviolent civil disobedience. That happening will be the beginning of the renewal of American democracy.

PRESIDENT OBAMA AND NONVIOLENT PEACE ACTIVISM

Many activists were particularly disturbed when President Obama, in his recent Nobel Peace Prize acceptance speech, made comments about the limits of nonviolence and the occasional necessity of war. To peace and justice activists, those remarks were devastating. Ken Butigan, a teacher of nonviolence with the Franciscan group *Pace e Bene*, eloquently stated, "that those of us who are convinced that creative nonviolence is an unparalleled force for constructive and lasting peace and justice have fallen down on the job. In the end, we have not sufficiently dramatized and communicated the news that that nonviolence is proving itself a powerful and effective alternate to both violence and passivity. President Obama is able so matter-of-factly to discredit nonviolence— and thus buttress his argument for war—because there is no sturdy conviction in the mind of the larger public that nonviolence is anything but limited, weak, passive, utopian, and effective." Butigan concluded, "Just as we have gradually mainstreamed the rule of law, human rights, and the vision of democracy, we have the opportunity to mainstream the power of creative nonviolence."

Peace activist and author Father John Dear, SJ, commented on the Oslo speech in his "On the Road to Peace" column in the *National Catholic Reporter*, December 15, 2009. He stated that President Obama's speech "undermined the example of all the peacemakers of the ages. Standing before the world, President Obama defended America's military misadventures, dismissed nonviolence and endorsed the just- war theory as a way to peace."

"The peacemakers Mahatma Gandhi and Dr. Martin Luther King Jr. received particular attention. With a kind of sleight of hand, Obama admired and scorned them at the same time, saying in effect: here are good men but, in our modern world, impractical men. With that, Obama undercut his own soaring campaign rhetoric espousing audacious hope. Hope withered on the moment. Here is another president beating the drums of war in the name of peace. Nothing makes the heart sink like the notion, a very Orwellian nightmare: "the way to peace is through war." His speech was a veritable call to despair." The emerging Christianity movement should reassert its faith in the power of nonviolent civil disobedience to bring about much needed radical social change."

THE LIMITS OF POWER

The Limits of Power: The End of American Exceptionalism, by Andrew J. Bacevich, is a powerful critique of American militarism. Andrew Bacevich is a retired U.S. Army colonel, a West Point graduate, a highly decorated Vietnam veteran, and now a professor of international relations at Boston University. Reading this book was like opening the window to clear out the smokescreen of American hubris and delusions of greatness. Andrew Bacevich's book is nothing less than the fresh air of honesty that is so lacking in the American mainstream media.

Andrew Bacevich begins by mourning the lost opportunities for peace after the Cold War. "Instead, the U.S. found this as an opportune time to expand and perpetuate the American Empire. In this expansion of the American Empire, the American people saw themselves as peaceful people and the conflicts in which they became involved were seen not of their own making." The current global war on terror has been no exception. To quote Bacevich, "Certain of our own benign intentions, we reflexively assign responsibility for war to others, typically malignant Hitler-like figures inexplicitly bent on denying us the peace that is our fondest wish." The *Limits of Power* challenges this worldview extensively.

To Bacevich, at the heart of this American blindness is the sense of American "freedom" and the American consumer way of life. This blindness is the perfect, fertile ground for government propaganda. The resulting sense of entitlement has great implications for American foreign policy. To quote Bacevich, "Simply put, as the American appetite for freedom has grown, so too has our penchant for empire." He reasons that "in an earlier age, Americans saw empire as the antithesis of freedom. Today with America's efforts to dominate the energy rich Persian Gulf, empire has seemingly become a prerequisite of freedom."

Andrew Bacevich sees the war against terrorism as an unending global war that cannot succeed. He has these wise words: "Americans ought to give up the presumptuous notion that they are called upon to tutor Muslims in matters related to freedom and the proper relationship between politics and religion. The principle informing policy should be this: Let islam be Islam, In the end, Muslims will have to discover for themselves the shortcomings of political Islam, much as Russians discovered the defects of Marxism-Leninism and the Chinese came to appreciate the flaws of Maoism even as ourselves will one day begin to recognize the snares embedded in American exceptionalism."

Andrew Bacevich also authored *The New American Militarism: How Americans Are Seduced by War*, *The Long War*, *A New History of U.S. National Security Policy since World War II*, and *American Empire: The Realities and Consequences of U.S. Diplomacy*.

SCAPEGOATS FOR WAR

Military power needs an enemy in order to sustain public support. So the religion of Islam has been made the scapegoat for war. To the ruling powers that be, the evil of Islam must be destroyed by the forces of goodness. This is the Manichean mindset, the oldest and most successful form of propaganda in the history of the world. Considering there are 1.3 billion Muslims in the world, this strategy is destined to be a highly profitable challenge for the U.S. defense industry. The war on terrorism is the new Cold War.

CONTINUING TO DWELL ON THE TRAGEDY OF 9/11

In the meantime, most Americans continue to dwell on the tragedy of 9/11. This is unfortunate. Many of the scholars in the world (notably Chalmers Johnson in his trilogy book series *Blowback*) conclude that 9/11 was pure "blowback" from American foreign policy. If Americans want a more peaceful world, then American foreign policy must change. But this will not be an easy task, even with a renewed democracy. There is fear among scholars that the United States is now addicted to a war economy. The reality is now sinking in—with so many manufacturing jobs relocated abroad, many of the best remaining manufacturing jobs in America are with the defense industry. To Americans, these jobs need to be protected at all costs, and thus the cycle for war continues. America is fast becoming a military nation. The emerging Christianity movement should be speaking about this militarization of our economy and our culture.

THE NEW WORLD ORDER: THE WORLD ECONOMIC FORUM MEETS IN DAVOS, SWITZERLAND

The best current description of events in Davos was recently written by Rachel Hope Anderson of the Center for Responsible Lending and published on the blog "God's Politics" by Jim Wallis of *Sojourners* magazine (02-01-2010). I am including her essay in full.

WHO HAS THE EARS TO HEAR AT DAVOS
BY RACHEL ANDERSON

Each year, over one thousand global leaders gather at a retreat center in Davos, Switzerland, to discuss the major economic, political, and technological forces currently at work in the world. Top executives from Google, HSBC, Archer Daniels Midland (ADM), JP Morgan Chase, Bank of America, and Morgan Stanley all gathered in Davos (officially titled the World Economic Forum) last week.

This is an elite group of leaders with almost mind-boggling capacity to impact the global economy and, hence, the lives of millions. Little demonstrates this better than the fact that the decisions by the very same financial corporations represented at Davos helped bring about the economic crisis that plummeted struggling nations into deeper poverty and many Americans into joblessness and foreclosure.

Providentially, faith and values were on the agenda this year. The Forum commissioned a poll and a report on "Values in the Post-Crisis Economy." More than 130,000 people from across the world weighed in via facebook and 15 global faith leaders offered reflections. Unsurprisingly, two-thirds of people surveyed believe the economic crisis is also a crisis of ethics and values. These faith leaders from the Christian, Buddhist, Jewish, and Muslim communities offered a tremendously profound and challenging perspective on what brought the world to economic disaster and what's now required of the global community.

In his address at Davos and his recent book *Rediscovering VALUES On Wall Street, and Your Street,* Jim Wallis has been encouraging everyone to **ask the right questions**. In their report on post-crisis values, many religious thinkers also sought to remind Davos participants of the *right* *purpose* of the economic sphere. Economic and financial activity is not an end in itself, but an instrument that must be guided to the benefit of people and the common good, many wrote. Dr. Lesley-Anne Knight, General Secretary of Caritas, a confederation of Catholic agencies, describes exactly how the global economy went off the rails over the last decade when detached from moral purpose.

> What was clearly lacking in the strategies and decisions that led to the crisis was any concept of respect for the human person. Attention was focused on financial mechanisms, profits, bonuses—anything but the human beings at whose doors the trail of disaster ended: poor people largely, people who had been given loans they would struggle to repay and who would subsequently lose their meager savings and homes as a result.

> Similarly, less that a year ago, Pope Benedict invited those in the financial sector to remember the ethical foundations of their work.

> I cannot help but ask whether all this faith-rooted wisdom transformed hearts in Davos. If, as

Jesus teaches, receptivity to truth has a great deal to do with the listeners' readiness to hear ("Those who have ears to hear, let them hear," he said) I can't help but wonder what kind of listening took place in Switzerland last week.

Among the Davos observers, many adopted a cynical stance toward the proceedings. Some report an atmosphere of self-congratulation within the financial sector and continued blindness to the impact of their excesses on the welfare of the globe. Others note a tinge of self-pity, citing a financial executive who complained, "tobacco companies have it so easy by comparison." Although reporters also suggested that participants adopted a humbler tone at the event's conclusion, acknowledging the cost of the financial crisis in loss of trust.

Pragmatically, I don't expect executives to leave Davos radically transformed. But I do believe and pray that God's spirit moves in mysterious and challenging ways. I also believe God's spirit can move through us as we lift up the questions that faith leaders posed at Davos so that when the time comes, those who have ears will hear.

THE DANGEROUS WORD CRUSADE

In his book *Crusade, Chronicles of An Unjust War*, James Carroll points out how, after 9/11, President George W. Bush II's inadvertent use of the term *crusade* was more than a slip of the tongue. It expressed Bush's exact truth, revealing his most deeply felt purpose. He defined *crusade* as *war*. Even offhandedly, he had said exactly what he meant. In doing so, he played into the hands of Osama bin Laden. His usage would set the West and Christianity against Islam. He opened old wounds from the bloody Christian crusades against Muslims one thousand years ago. James Carroll stated, "Americans do not know what fire they are playing with. Osama Bin Laden, however, knows all too well, and in his periodic pronouncements, he uses the world 'crusade' to this day, as a flamethrower."

To James Carroll, this war against terrorism has led to a cosmic battle between the transcendent forces of good and evil. "Such a battle becomes unlimited and justifies radical actions—the abandonment of established notions of civic justice at home and of traditional alliances abroad. The fervor of Christianity was starkly joined to America's new purpose." However, James Carroll emphasizes, "When humans go to war, God in no way wills it."

Allow me to quote James Carroll's summarizing paragraph: "There is no crime of which Muslims acting as Muslims have been accused that Christians, to cite only one other religion, do not also stand accused by history. To be religious is, first, to be repentant. The danger of a 'clash of civilizations,' or even of a new holy war between the remnants of a Christian West and 'the Islamic World,' will be far less if we all understand that we are alike as human beings. Our noblest impulses come inevitably intertwined with opposite inclinations that betray them. We religious humans must constantly submit to the judgment of history, practicing self-criticism, always seeking the reform that will draw us closer to our best ideals. Certainly Islam is engaged in such a reckoning today. But this task belongs to all religious people—the only way to honor God and love our neighbors as ourselves."

James Carroll is a columnist for the *Boston Globe.* His most renowned work is *An American Requiem: Constantine's Sword*, a history of Christian anti-Semitism, and ten other books.

CHRISTIANITY AND ISLAM TORN BY FUNDAMENTALISM

The world is not as divided as much by religion as it appears. The problem stems mainly from deep conflicts within both Christianity and Islam. In America, a small minority of conservative Christian fundamentalists, including a number of Catholics, believe in an authoritarian God, a vengeful God. They also have been seduced by the "gospel of prosperity" that considers personal wealth a blessing from God. Christian fundamentalists love religious absolutes and religious authority. It seems that Christian fundamentalists have become the great protectors of capitalism and the great patriots who wage war against imagined evil. However, the vast majority of Christians in America believe in a compassionate, peace loving, and forgiving God. They do not believe in the theory of "preventative war" and believe in democracy for the common good.

Likewise, in the Islamic world, a few radical fundamentalists are quick to rise up against the "infidels" of the West. This kind of radicalism is featured on television often. However, the vast majority of Muslims do not condone violence.

However, moderate Muslims are certainly threatened by the Western culture of decadent consumer capitalism and by multinational corporations seeking to control their nations' oil resources. They also feel threatened by the presence of foreign troops on Islamic soil and by American foreign policy.

What we have here are the minority forces of religious fundamentalism dominating national political discourse. In most cases, American bishops and pastors and Islamic mullahs in the Middle East have seriously failed to condemn war and the killing of innocent civilians sufficiently to influence a shift in public dialogue and national policies.

WHO'S TERRORISM?

Foreign Policy in Focus published an article by Eric Stoner on December 17, 2009. I would like to quote two paragraphs from the article.

In his book, *Dying to Win: The Strategy Logic of Suicide Terrorism*, University of Chicago professor Robert Page created a database on every suicide bombing from 1980 to 2004. Page found that, rather than being driven by religion, the vast majority of suicide bombers—responsible for over 95% of all incidents on record—were primarily motivated by a desire to compel a democratic government to withdraw its military forces from land they saw as their homeland.

Since suicide terrorism is mainly a response to foreign occupation and not Islamic fundamentalism," Page said in an interview with *The American Conservative*, "the use of heavy military force to transform Muslim societies over there, if you would, is only likely to increase the number of suicide terrorists coming at us."

WHERE SHOULD THE EMERGING CHRISTIANITY MOVEMENT BE ON THE ISSUE OF ISLAMIC TERRORISM?

I believe it is time for Christianity and Islam to come together within the common bonds of sacred energies and speak boldly against the oppression and insanity of Western corporate capitalism. This will take much energy on the part of millions of like-minded Christians and Muslims. Now I ask: Will the Catholic Church rise to the challenge? To be optimistic, all people of all religions want a better world and a more promising life for their families. Accordingly, followers of Islam and of Christianity need to recognize that their own promising future lies in coming together for universal justice. They need to rally support for universal justice through the United Nations and a reinvigorated International World Court. Only a powerful alliance between Christianity and Islam can make universal justice a reality.

A MAJOR STUMBLING BLOCK

In *Future Church*, John L. Allen points out that "there is a bitter intra-Catholic theological divide between those who stress the activity of the Holy Spirit outside the visible bounds of Christianity and those who insist upon the singularity of Christ and the Church." He stresses the gravity of the divide: "It has been the most agonizing subject in Catholicism for the past two decades." He also stresses the consequences of the divide: "Catholicism's best minds on Islam, for example, probably spend at least as much time arguing with one another as they do actually talking to

Muslims, or helping to guide the discussion of Islam in the West in productive directions." I hope the emerging Christianity movement might be able to play a role in the resolution of these issues through its powerful spirit of synthesis.

In summary, in order to engage all humankind, universal justice, human rights, and democracy should be the major focus of the emerging Christianity movement. The freedom to think great thoughts will give much credibility to the emerging Christianity movement.

COMMENCEMENT ADDRESS BY PRESIDENT JOHN F. KENNEDY AT AMERICAN UNIVERSITY IN WASHINGTON, D.C. ON JUNE 10, 1963

President Anderson, members of the faculty, board of trustees, distinguished guests, my old colleague, Senator Bob Byrd, who has earned his degree through many years of attending night law school, while I am earning mine in the next thirty minutes, distinguished guests, ladies and gentlemen:

It is with great pride that I participate in this ceremony of the American University, sponsored by the Methodist Church, founded by Bishop John Fletcher Hurst, and first opened by President Woodrow Wilson in 1914. This is a young and growing university, but it has already fulfilled Bishop Hurst's enlightened hope for the study of history and public affairs in a city devoted to the making of history and the conduct of the public's business. By sponsoring this institution of higher learning for all who wish to learn, whatever their color or their creed, the Methodists of this area and the Nation deserve the Nation's thanks, and I commend all those who are today graduating.

Professor Woodrow Wilson once said that every man sent out from a university should be a man of his nation as well as a man of his time, and I am confident that the men and women who carry the honor of graduating from this institution will continue to give from their lives, from their talents, a high measure of public service and public support.

"There are few earthly things more beautiful than a university," wrote John Masefield in his tribute to English universities—and his words are equally true today. He did not refer to spires and towers, to campus greens and ivied walls. He admired the splendid beauty of the university, he said, because it was "a place where those who hate ignorance may strive to know, where those who perceive truth may strive to make others see."

I have, therefore, chosen this time and this place to discuss a topic on which ignorance too often abounds and the truth is too rarely perceived—yet it is the most important topic on earth: world peace.

What kind of peace do I mean? What kind of peace do we seek? Not a Pax Americana enforced on the world by American weapons of war. Not the peace of the grave or the security of the slave. I am talking about genuine peace, the kind of peace that makes life on earth worth living, the kind that enables men and nations to grow and to hope and to build a better life for their children— not merely peace for Americans but peace for all men and women—not merely peace in our time but peace for all time.

I speak of peace because of the new face of war. Total war makes no sense in an age when great powers can maintain large and relatively invulnerable nuclear forces and refuse to surrender without resort to those forces. It makes no sense in an age when a single nuclear weapon contains almost ten times the explosive force delivered by all the allied air forces in the Second World War. It makes no sense in an age when the deadly poisons produced by a nuclear exchange would be carried by wind and water and soil and seed to the far corners of the globe and to generations yet unborn.

Today the expenditure of billions of dollars every year on weapons acquired for the purpose of making sure we never need to use them is essential to keeping the peace. But surely the acquisition of such idle stockpiles—which can only destroy and never create—is not the only, much less the most efficient, means of assuring peace.

I speak of peace, therefore, as the necessary rational end of rational men. I realize that the pursuit of peace is not as dramatic as the pursuit of war—and frequently the words of the pursuer fall on deaf ears. But we have no more urgent task.

Some say that it is useless to speak of world peace or world law or world disarmament--and that it will be useless until the leaders of the Soviet Union adopt a more enlightened attitude. I hope they do. I believe we can help them do it. But

I also believe that we must reexamine our own attitude—as individuals and as a Nation—for our attitude is as essential as theirs. And every graduate of this school, every thoughtful citizen who despairs of war and wishes to bring peace, should begin by looking inward—by examining his own attitude toward the possibilities of peace, toward the Soviet Union, toward the course of the cold war and toward freedom and peace here at home.

First: Let us examine our attitude toward peace itself. Too many of us think it is impossible. Too many think it unreal. But that is a dangerous, defeatist belief. It leads to the conclusion that war is inevitable—that mankind is doomed—that we are gripped by forces we cannot control.

We need not accept that view. Our problems are manmade—therefore, they can be solved by man. And man can be as big as he wants. No problem of human destiny is beyond human beings. Man's reason and spirit have often solved the seemingly unsolvable—and we believe they can do it again.

I am not referring to the absolute, infinite concept of peace and goos but we merely invite discouragement and incredulity by making that our only and immediate goal.

Let us focus instead on a more practical, more attainable peace— based not on a sudden revolution in human nature but on a gradual evolution in human institutions—on a series of concrete actions and effective agreements which are in the interest of all concerned. There is no single, simple key to this peace—no grand or magic formula to be adopted by one or two powers. Genuine peace must be the product of many nations, the sum of many acts. It must be dynamic, not static, changing to meet the challenge of each new generation. For peace is a process—a way of solving problems.

With such a peace, there will still be quarrels and conflicting interests, as there are within families and nations. World peace, like community peace, does not require that each man love his neighbor—it requires only that they live together in mutual tolerance, submitting their disputes to a just and peaceful settlement. And history teaches us that enmities between nations, as between individuals, do not last forever. However fixed our likes and dislikes may seem, the tide of time and events will often bring surprising changes in the relations between nations and neighbors.

So let us persevere. Peace need not be impracticable, and war need not be inevitable. By defining our goal more clearly, by making it seem more manageable and less remote, we can help all peoples to see it, to draw hope from it, and to move irresistibly toward it.

Second: Let us reexamine our attitude toward the Soviet Union. It is discouraging to think that their leaders may actually believe what their propagandists write. It is discouraging to read a recent authoritative Soviet text on Military Strategy and find, on page after page, wholly baseless and incredible claims—such as the allegation that "American imperialist circles are preparing to unleash different types of wars ... that there is a very real threat of a preventive war being unleashed by American imperialists against the Soviet Union ... [and that] the political aims of the American imperialists are to enslave economically and politically the European and other capitalist countries ... [and] to achieve world domination ... by means of aggressive wars."

Truly, as it was written long ago: "The wicked flee when no man pursueth." Yet it is sad to read these Soviet statements—to realize the extent of the gulf between us. But it is also a warning—a warning to the American people not to fall into the same trap as the Soviets, not to see only a distorted and desperate view of the other side, not to see conflict as inevitable, accommodation as impossible, and communication as nothing more than an exchange of threats.

No government or social system is so evil that its people must be considered as lacking in virtue. As Americans, we find communism profoundly repugnant as a negation of personal freedom and dignity. But we can still hail the Russian people for their many achievements—in science and space, in economic and industrial growth, in culture and in acts of courage.

Among the many traits the peoples of our two countries have in common, none is stronger than our mutual abhorrence of war. Almost unique among the major world powers, we have never been at war with each other. And no nation in the history of battle ever suffered more than the Soviet Union suffered in the course of the Second World War. At least 20 million lost their lives.

Countless millions of homes and farms were burned or sacked. A third of the nation's territory, including nearly two thirds of its industrial base, was turned into a wasteland—a loss equivalent to the devastation of this country east of Chicago.

Today, should total war ever break out again—no matter how—our two countries would become the primary targets. It is an ironic but accurate fact that the two strongest powers are the two in the most danger of devastation. All we have built, all we have worked for, would be destroyed in the first twenty-four hours. And even in the cold war, which brings burdens and dangers to so many nations, including this Nation's closest allies—our two countries bear the heaviest burdens. For we are both devoting massive sums of money to weapons that could be better devoted to combating ignorance, poverty, and disease. We are both caught up in a vicious and dangerous cycle in which suspicion on one side breeds suspicion on the other, and new weapons beget counterweapons.

In short, both the United States and its allies, and the Soviet Union and its allies, have a mutually deep interest in a just and genuine peace and in halting the arms race. Agreements to this end are in the interests of the Soviet Union as well as ours—and even the most hostile nations can be relied upon to accept and keep those treaty obligations, and only those treaty obligations, which are in their own interest.

So, let us not be blind to our differences—but let us also direct attention to our common interests and to the means by which those differences can be resolved. And if we cannot end now our differences, at least we can help make the world safe for diversity. For, in the final analysis, our most basic common link is that we all inhabit this small planet. We all breathe the same air. We all cherish our children's future. And we are all mortal.

Third: Let us reexamine our attitude toward the cold war, remembering that we are not engaged in a debate, seeking to pile up debating points. We are not here distributing blame or pointing the finger of judgment. We must deal with the world as it is, and not as it might have been had the history of the last eighteen years been different.

We must, therefore, persevere in the search for peace in the hope that constructive changes within the Communist bloc might bring within reach solutions which now seem beyond us. We must conduct our affairs in such a way that it becomes in the Communists' interest to agree on a genuine peace. Above all, while defending our own vital interests, nuclear powers must avert those confrontations which bring an adversary to a choice of either a humiliating retreat or a nuclear war. To adopt that kind of course in the nuclear age would be evidence only of the bankruptcy of our policy—or of a collective death-wish for the world.

To secure these ends, America's weapons are nonprovocative, carefully controlled, designed to deter, and capable of selective use. Our military forces are committed to peace and disciplined in self-restraint. Our diplomats are instructed to avoid unnecessary irritants and purely rhetorical hostility.

For we can seek a relaxation of tension without relaxing our guard. And, for our part, we do not need to use threats to prove that we are resolute. We do not need to jam foreign broadcasts out of fear our faith will be eroded. We are unwilling to impose our system on any unwilling people—but we are willing and able to engage in peaceful competition with any people on earth.

Meanwhile, we seek to strengthen the United Nations, to help solve its financial problems, to make it a more effective instrument for peace, to develop it into a genuine world security system—a system capable of resolving disputes on the basis of law, of insuring the security of the large and the small, and of creating conditions under which arms can finally be abolished.

At the same time we seek to keep peace inside the non-Communist world, where many nations, all of them our friends, are divided over issues which weaken Western unity, which invite Communist intervention or which threaten to erupt into war. Our efforts in West New Guinea, in the Congo, in the Middle East, and in the Indian subcontinent, have been persistent and patient despite criticism from both sides. We have also tried to set an example for others—by seeking to adjust small but significant differences with our own closest neighbors in Mexico and in Canada.

Speaking of other nations, I wish to make one point clear. We are bound to many nations by alliances. Those alliances exist because our concern and theirs substantially overlap. Our commitment to defend Western Europe and West Berlin, for example, stands undiminished because of the identity of our vital interests. The United States will make no deal with the Soviet Union at the expense of other nations and other peoples, not merely because they are our partners, but also because their interests and ours converge.

Our interests converge, however, not only in defending the frontiers of freedom, but in pursuing the paths of peace. It is our hope—and the purpose of allied policies—to convince the Soviet Union that she, too, should let each nation choose its own future, so long as that choice does not interfere with the choices of others. The Communist drive to impose their political and economic system on others is the primary cause of world tension today. For there can be no doubt that, if all nations could refrain from interfering in the self-determination of others, the peace would be much more assured.

This will require a new effort to achieve world law—a new context for world discussions. It will require increased understanding between the Soviets and ourselves. And increased understanding will require increased contact and communication. One step in this direction is the proposed arrangement for a direct line between Moscow and Washington, to avoid on each side the dangerous delays, misunderstandings, and misreadings of the other's actions which might occur at a time of crisis.

We have also been talking in Geneva about the other first-step measures of arms control designed to limit the intensity of the arms race and to reduce the risks of accidental war. Our primary long range interest in Geneva, however, is general and complete disarmament—designed to take place by stages, permitting parallel political developments to build the new institutions of peace which would take the place of arms. The pursuit of disarmament has been an effort of this Government since the 1920s. It has been urgently sought by the past three administrations. And however dim the prospects may be today, we intend to continue this effort—to continue it in order that all countries, including our own, can better grasp what the problems and possibilities of disarmament are.

The one major area of these negotiations where the end is in sight, yet where a fresh start is badly needed, is in a treaty to outlaw nuclear tests. The conclusion of such a treaty, so near and yet so far, would check the spiraling arms race in one of its most dangerous areas. It would place the nuclear powers in a position to deal more effectively with one of the greatest hazards which man faces in 1963, the further spread of nuclear arms. It would increase our security—it would decrease the prospects of war. Surely this goal is sufficiently important to require our steady pursuit, yielding neither to the temptation to give up the whole effort nor the temptation to give up our insistence on vital and responsible safeguards.

I am taking this opportunity, therefore, to announce two important decisions in this regard.

First: Chairman Khrushchev, Prime Minister Macmillan, and I have agreed that high-level discussions will shortly begin in Moscow looking toward early agreement on a comprehensive test ban treaty. Our hopes must be tempered with the caution of history—but with our hopes go the hopes of all mankind.

Second: To make clear our good faith and solemn convictions on the matter, I now declare that the United States does not propose to conduct nuclear tests in the atmosphere so long as other states do not do so. We will not be the first to resume. Such a declaration is no substitute for a formal binding treaty, but I hope it will help us achieve one. Nor would such a treaty be a substitute for disarmament, but I hope it will help us achieve it.

Finally, my fellow Americans, let us examine our attitude toward peace and freedom here at home. The quality and spirit of our own society must justify and support our efforts abroad. We must show it in the dedication of our own lives—as many of you who are graduating today will have a unique opportunity to do, by serving without pay in the Peace Corps abroad or in the proposed National Service Corps here at home.

But wherever we are, we must all, in our daily lives, live up to the age-old faith that peace and freedom walk together. In too many of our cities today, the peace is not secure because the freedom is incomplete.

It is the responsibility of the executive branch at all levels of government—local, State, and National—to provide and protect that freedom for all of our citizens by all means within their authority. It is the responsibility of the legislative branch at all levels, wherever that authority is not now adequate, to make it adequate. And it is the responsibility of all citizens in all sections of this country to respect the rights of all others and to respect the law of the land.

All this is not unrelated to world peace. "When a man's ways please the Lord," the Scriptures tell us, "he maketh even his enemies to be at peace with him." And is not peace, in the last analysis, basically a matter of human rights—the right to live out our lives without fear of devastation--the right to breathe air as nature provided it—the right of future generations to a healthy existence?

While we proceed to safeguard our national interests, let us also safeguard human interests. And the elimination of war and arms is clearly in the interest of both. No treaty, however much it may be to the advantage of all, however tightly it may be worded, can provide absolute security against the risks of deception and evasion. But it can—if it is sufficiently effective in its enforcement and if it is sufficiently in the interests of its signers— offer far more security and far fewer risks than an unabated, uncontrolled, unpredictable arms race.

The United States, as the world knows, will never start a war. We do not want a war. We do not now expect a war. This generation of Americans has already had enough—more than enough—of war and hate and oppression. We shall be prepared if others wish it. We shall be alert to try to stop it. But we shall also do our part to build a world of peace where the weak are safe and the strong are just. We are not helpless before that task or hopeless of its success. Confident and unafraid, we labor on—not toward a strategy of annihilation but toward a strategy of peace.

THE SPIRITUAL JOURNEY OF STEPHEN V. RILEY

Steve is recently widowed (July 1, 2006) after forty-four years of marriage to Deborah M. Riley, "the love of his life forever." Born in Quincy, Massachusetts, Steve graduated from Boston College in 1956 and served two years as a junior officer in the Infantry Center at Fort Benning, Georgia.

Steve and his wife Deborah were the builders and proprietors of the Black Bear Lodge in the Bolton Valley Ski Area, Bolton, Vermont, from 1968 to 1979.

In 1979 Steve and his family moved to Sarasota, Florida. In Sarasota, he was active in peace and justice issues. His activities included facilitating, for three years, a course on structural injustice that he had developed with the Peace and Justice Ministry of Incarnation Parish. In Florida, Steve was also active with Pax Christi Florida and the Nader 2000 Green Party campaign; he was an advocate for the Earth Charter initiative and a familiar contributor of Letters to the Editor in the *Sarasota Herald Tribune*.

In 1999 Steve attended the WTO demonstrations in Seattle, Washington, and the World Bank demonstrations in Washington, DC. In both Seattle and Washington, DC, he attended teach-ins by the International Forum on Globalization.

It was on October 10, 2001, that Steve submitted a thirty-two-page open letter to the three hundred and two American Catholic bishops, entitled "The American Challenge and a New Catholic Awareness." In this paper, Steve critiqued the lack of critical social analysis in local diocesan Catholic newspapers and the similar absence of a true "civic press" in the American mainstream news media. To fill this void, Steve suggested the formation of a Catholic "progressive think tank" to be a resource of essential critical social analysis for Catholic regional newspapers. In addition, Steve provided the American bishops with an assessment of the Earth Charter and challenged them to endorse the Earth Charter for ratification by the United Nations.

After the loss of his wife Deborah in 2006, Steve moved to Tahoe City, California, to be with his daughter, Dr. Stephenie V. Riley ND, and family and son Allen Riley, a professional skier and with the Squaw Valley Fire Department. Steve joined St. Francis of Assisi Parish in Incline Village, Nevada. There he cofacilitated an eight-month social justice program, Just Faith, founded by Jack Jezreel of Louisville, Kentucky.

In September 2006, Steve participated in the five-day Thomas Merton-Gandhi walk from the Thomas Merton Hermitage at the Abbey of Gethsemane to Louisville, Kentucky, led by Father John Dear, S.J. This ecumenical walk honored the anniversaries of the nonviolence activism of both Mahatma Gandhi and Thomas Merton.

Since 2006 Steve has attended numerous conferences led by Franciscan Father Richard Rohr of the Center for Action and Contemplation in Albuquerque, New Mexico. One such conference was the ecumenical Emerging Church Conference in 2009. Steve has also been a frequent poster on the progressive web site Common Dreams. Steve has written thirteen book reviews on Amazon. com, including a review of his favorite, *Shaking the Gates of Hell: Faith-led Resistance to Globalization*, by Sharon Delgado.

In July of 2008, Steve flew to Chicago and rented a van to be a support vehicle for the first two weeks of the witness against war 2008 walk from Chicago to the Republican Convention in St. Paul, Minnesota. This 450-mile walk was led by world-renowned peace activist and Noble Peace Prize Nominee Kathy Kelly.

In 2009 Steve attended the Sophia Summer Institute in Berkeley, California. The Sophia Institute teaches the cosmic spirituality of Father Thomas Berry. In 2009 Steve also attended the *Pace e Bene* twentieth-year anniversary conference in Las Vegas. The *Pace e Bene* conference concluded with "witness in the desert" demonstrations led by longtime activist Franciscan Father Louie Vitale. The demonstration was held at Creech Air Force Base, where the U.S. military controls the pilotless drones by computer, and also at the Nevada Atomic Test Site.

In October of 2009, Steve attended the economics of peace conference sponsored by the Praxis Peace Institute and RSF Social Finance in Sonoma, California. This conference dealt with alternate systems of local business and local independent banks providing financing secured by local real wealth. Also there was a presentation by two executives from the Mondragon worker-owned and -managed cooperatives in the Basque country of Spain.

You can feel free to contact Steve Riley at PO Box 5364, Tahoe City, CA or by e-mail: stephenvriley@hotmail.com.

www.ingramcontent.com/pod-product-compliance
Lightning Source LLC
Chambersburg PA
CBHW030410290526
45785CB00004B/1953